Piano Accompaniment

GERSHWIN

By Special Arrangement

Eleven Songs by
George Gershwin®
Arranged by **CARL STROMMEN**
Jazz-Style Arrangements
With a "Variation"

CONTENTS

GERSHWIN® and GEORGE GERSHWIN®
are registered trademarks of Gershwin Enterprises
All Rights Reserved

Project Manager: Thom Proctor
Jazz Consultant: Pete BarenBregge
Production Coordinator: Maudlyn Cooley
Art Design: Thais Yanes
Engraver: Adrian Alvarez
CD Producer: Teena Chinn
Recording Engineer: Kendall Thomsen
Recorded at Starke Lake Studios

WARNER BROS. PUBLICATIONS - THE GLOBAL LEADER IN PRINT
USA: 15800 NW 48th Avenue, Miami, FL 33014

WARNER/CHAPPELL MUSIC
CANADA: 15800 N.W. 48th AVENUE
MIAMI, FLORIDA 33014
SCANDINAVIA: P.O. BOX 533, VENDEVAGEN 85 B
S-182 15, DANDERYD, SWEDEN
AUSTRALIA: P.O. BOX 353
3 TALAVERA ROAD, NORTH RYDE N.S.W. 2113
ASIA: UNIT 901 - LIPPO SUN PLAZA
28 CANTON ROAD
TSIM SHA TSUI, KOWLOON, HONG KONG

NUOVA CARISCH
ITALY: VIA CAMPANIA, 12
20098 S. GIULIANO MILANESE (MI)
ZONA INDUSTRIALE SESTO ULTERIANO
SPAIN: MAGALLANES, 25
28015 MADRID
FRANCE: CARISCH MUSICOM,
25, RUE D'HAUTEVILLE, 75010 PARIS

IMP
INTERNATIONAL MUSIC PUBLICATIONS LIMITED
ENGLAND: GRIFFIN HOUSE,
161 HAMMERSMITH ROAD, LONDON W6 8BS
GERMANY: MARSTALLSTR. 8, D-80539 MUNCHEN
DENMARK: DANMUSIK, VOGNMAGERGADE 7
DK 1120 KOBENHAVNK

I GOT RHYTHM

Music and Lyrics by
GEORGE GERSHWIN and IRA GERSHWIN
Arranged by CARL STROMMEN

PIANO

Bright ♩ = 186

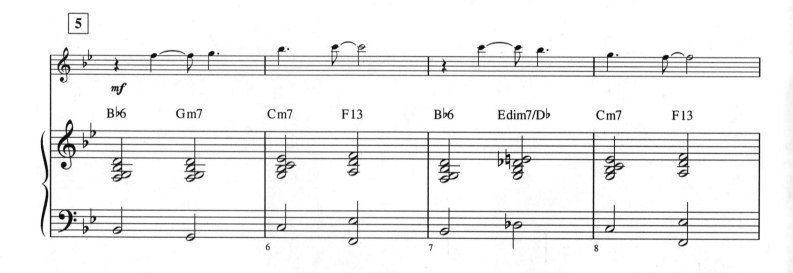

* Solos between the asterisks may vary from instrument to instrument.

0478B

0478B

BUT NOT FOR ME

Music and Lyrics by
GEORGE GERSHWIN and IRA GERSHWIN
Arranged by CARL STROMMEN

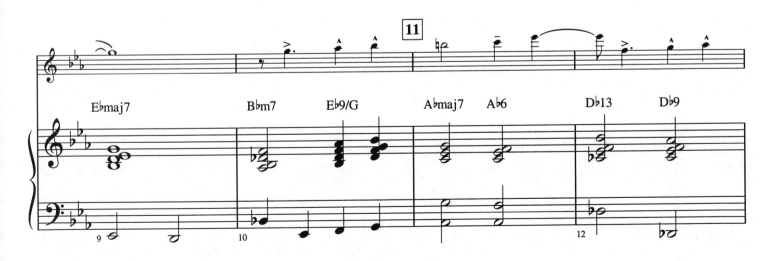

0478B

10

0478B

EMBRACEABLE YOU

Music and Lyrics by
GEORGE GERSHWIN and IRA GERSHWIN
Arranged by CARL STROMMEN

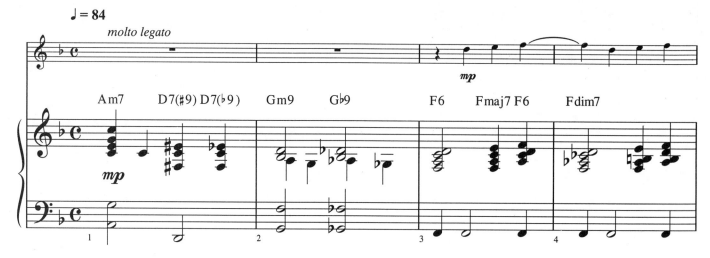

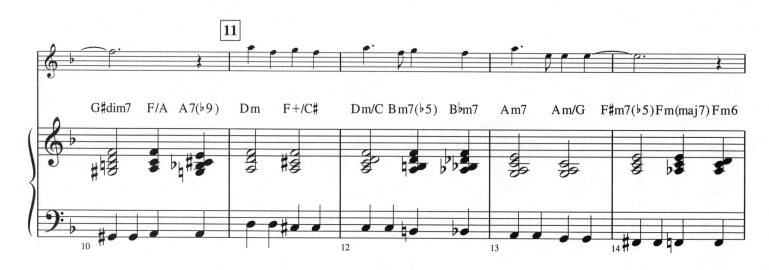

14

0478B

A FOGGY DAY

Music and Lyrics by
GEORGE GERSHWIN and IRA GERSHWIN
Arranged by CARL STROMMEN

Bright ♩ = 176

FASCINATING RHYTHM

Music and Lyrics by
GEORGE GERSHWIN and IRA GERSHWIN
Arranged by CARL STROMMEN

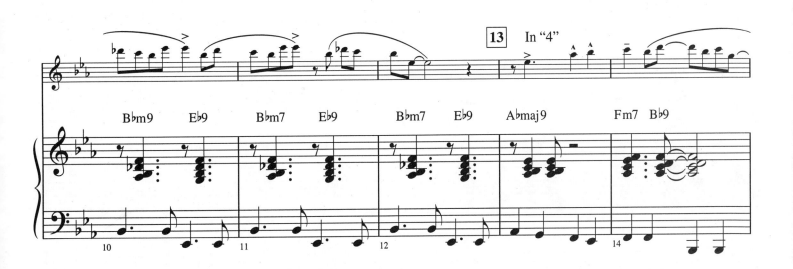

0478B

24

0478B

I'VE GOT A CRUSH ON YOU

Music and Lyrics by
GEORGE GERSHWIN and IRA GERSHWIN
Arranged by CARL STROMMEN

0478B

28

'S WONDERFUL

Music and Lyrics by
GEORGE GERSHWIN and IRA GERSHWIN
Arranged by CARL STROMMEN

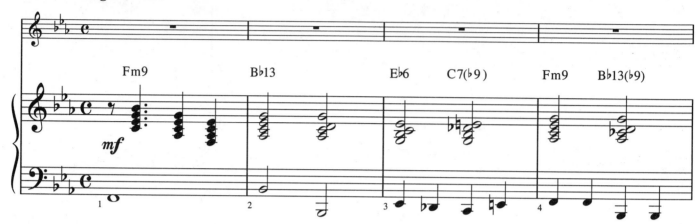

HOW LONG HAS THIS BEEN GOING ON

Music and Lyrics by
GEORGE GERSHWIN and IRA GERSHWIN
Arranged by CARL STROMMEN

0478B

NICE WORK IF YOU CAN GET IT

Music and Lyrics by
GEORGE GERSHWIN and **IRA GERSHWIN**
Arranged by CARL STROMMEN

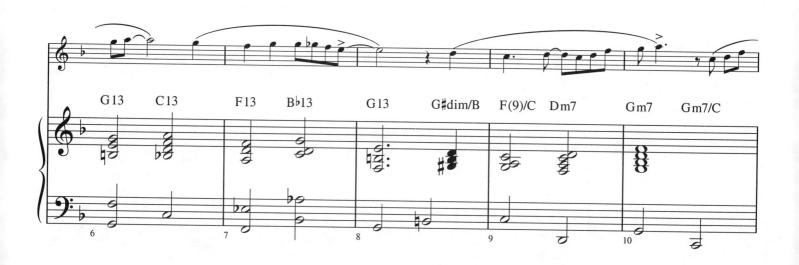

42

0478B

SOMEONE TO WATCH OVER ME

Music and Lyrics by
GEORGE GERSHWIN and IRA GERSHWIN
Arranged by CARL STROMMEN

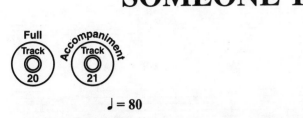

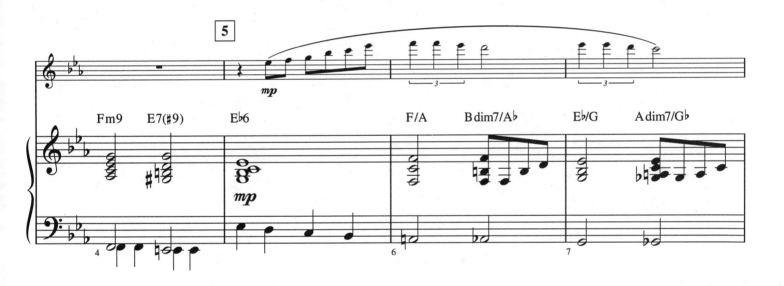

0478B

STRIKE UP THE BAND!

Music and Lyrics by
GEORGE GERSHWIN and IRA GERSHWIN
Arranged by CARL STROMMEN

0478B

HOW TO USE THIS BOOK

The piano parts are simplified transcriptions of the recorded accompaniment. The pianist is encouraged to embellish upon what is written, creatively and tastefully, and not to overpower the soloist. The introductions and endings should be played as written. The cued flute solo part above the piano part is included as a guide, or the pianist can use it to play the melody or written solo. The written improvised solos vary from instrument to instrument as indicated between the asterisks.

Because of the great melodies and rich chord progressions, the music of George Gershwin continues to be fertile ground for jazz players. The transcribed solos have been slightly altered to conform to a moderate degree of difficulty. The player should use the written solo section as a guide and a springboard to personal improvising efforts.

The nuances of the jazz style are impossible to notate exactly. Key to this style is the concept of the swing or syncopated rhythm. The treatment and interpretation of eighth notes largely contribute to this elusive feel. In rock or Latin-style music, eighth notes are played as written, evenly, with the accent on the downbeat:

Swing eighth notes are treated differently at different tempos, but they are usually written as even eighths. At moderate tempos, the figure would be played as . At bright tempos, the swing feel tends to flatten out and is played more evenly with the pulse on the second half of the beat.

Slower tempos (ballads) also tend to have a slightly more even eighth note feel. (Notice in listening to some solos that although the rhythm section is playing in a 12/8 feel, the solo is being played with even eighth notes.)

Players who are used to playing only in orchestral or wind ensemble settings have to make the adjustment of observing and interpreting eighth notes differently when placed in a big band or small group environment.

Some of the following unique jazz articulations are written out in these arrangements, but you can add more, tastefully, to create your own style.

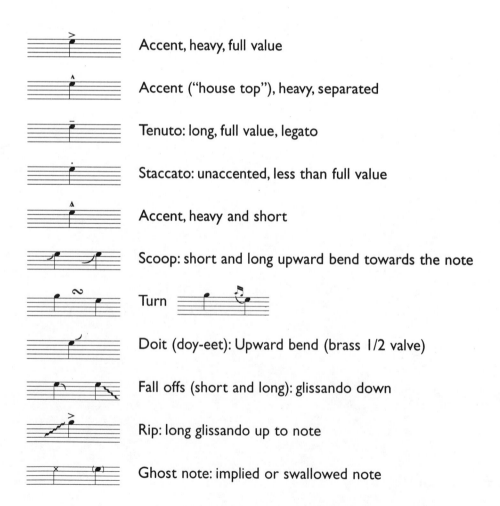

Accent, heavy, full value

Accent ("house top"), heavy, separated

Tenuto: long, full value, legato

Staccato: unaccented, less than full value

Accent, heavy and short

Scoop: short and long upward bend towards the note

Turn

Doit (doy-eet): Upward bend (brass 1/2 valve)

Fall offs (short and long): glissando down

Rip: long glissando up to note

Ghost note: implied or swallowed note

For more information and further study of improvisation, refer to the Jazz Improvisation Series books *Approaching the Standards* by Dr. Willie L. Hill, Jr., published by Warner Bros. Publications.